DIGITAL ALLCHEMIST

Industrial Robotics: Automation Beyond the PLC

Book 3 of 10 in the series

THE **DIGITAL**
ALLCHEMIST

Contents

1

Introduction

Introduction

This eBook is the third in the series, into industrial robotics, exploring how robots are integrated into manufacturing processes, the technologies behind them, and future trends in robotics and automation. By knowing these details, this guide provides enough foundation information for those who wish to consider a career in Robotics / Industrial Automation companies

About the Author

The Author has more than 30+ years of experience in the field of practical applications of Industrial Automation, IoT, MES, Industry Consulting for Manufacturing Organizations.

"Digital alchemy" is a state that a business can strive to achieve by using its assets and technology to redesign operations and innovate. This can help a business digitally transform itself.

2

Introduction to Industrial Robotics and Their Applications

What is Industrial Robotics?

Industrial robots are machines designed to handle tasks that are typically repetitive, dangerous, or require extreme precision. In modern manufacturing, robots are used to automate processes such as assembly, welding, painting, material handling, and quality inspection. The primary goal of using robots in manufacturing is to improve productivity, enhance quality, and reduce the risks associated with manual labor.

Case Study:

- **BMW Group** uses industrial robots extensively in its production lines. The company employs over 1,000 robots to carry out tasks like **painting, welding**, and **assembly** at its Leipzig plant. The robots work alongside human workers, enhancing productivity without compromising safety or flexibility.
- Key Applications of Industrial Robots

Automotive Manufacturing

- Industrial robots are widely used in automotive manufacturing for tasks such as **welding, painting, and assembly**.
- **Use Case**: **Tesla**'s **Model 3** production line is heavily automated, using robots for high-precision tasks such as **spot welding** and **installing parts**. The use of robots allows Tesla to meet high production volumes while ensuring consistent product quality.

Electronics and Consumer Goods

- In electronics, robots help with **PCB assembly**, **soldering**, and **quality control**.
- **Use Case**: **Foxconn**, a major manufacturer of consumer electronics, employs robots in the production of smartphones. Robots are used for tasks such as **screen assembly**, **welding** parts, and **testing** components, ensuring high precision and speed.

Pharmaceutical and Food Industry

- Robots in food manufacturing handle tasks such as **packaging, sorting, and palletizing**.
- **Use Case**: **KUKA** robots are used in the **Nestlé** factory in Switzerland to handle sensitive tasks like **packaging chocolate**. These robots improve packaging efficiency while ensuring that food safety standards are met.

Logistics and Warehousing

- **Amazon** uses robots extensively in its **fulfillment centers** to transport goods, pick orders, and sort packages.

Use Case: **Amazon Robotics**, formerly Kiva Systems, has transformed warehouse operations. Robots in Amazon's facilities autonomously transport goods to packing stations, significantly reducing human labor requirements

5

and improving inventory management.

Importance of Robotics in Modern Manufacturing

Industrial robots are pivotal to Industry 4.0, where automation and connectivity are transforming factories into **smart factories**. Robots contribute to increased efficiency, improved quality control, and reduced human errors.

3

Types of Industrial Robots

Articulated Robots

Description: Articulated robots, often referred to as **robot arms**, are one of the most versatile types of industrial robots. They consist of multiple rotational joints, which allow the arm to move in many directions and reach a wide range of points in 3D space. Articulated robots are often equipped with **end effectors** such as grippers or welding torches, depending on the task. Their high degrees of freedom make them ideal for applications that require flexibility, like **welding**, **assembly**, and **material handling**.

Key Features:

- **Degrees of freedom (DOF)**: Typically 4 to 6, allowing for complex movements and versatility.
- **Applications**: Welding, assembly, material handling, painting, and pick-and-place tasks.
- **Precision**: High precision in repetitive tasks, ensuring product quality.

Use Case:

- **General Motors** uses articulated robots in its **welding lines**. For example, the **KUKA KR 1000** is used for precise welding of car bodies. These robots can maneuver into tight spaces, execute multiple welding positions, and produce high-quality, consistent welds.

Career Tip:

- **Skills Needed**: Proficiency in **robot programming languages** like **KRL (KUKA Robot Language)** or **RAPID (ABB)**. Additionally, understanding **motion control**, **kinematics**, and **robot simulation software** (like **RoboDK**) is crucial.
- **Career Path**: Focus on industries like automotive manufacturing, aerospace, and heavy machinery where articulated robots are widely used for assembly, inspection, and welding.

SCARA Robots (Selective Compliance Assembly Robot Arm)

Description: SCARA robots are designed with **horizontal motion** capability and **vertical compliance**. They are rigid in the horizontal plane and flexible in the vertical, allowing them to perform highly precise tasks at high speeds. Their structure enables them to handle delicate components with high repeatability.

Key Features:

- **High Speed**: SCARA robots excel in high-speed tasks like **pick-and-place** and **packaging**.
- **Precision**: They offer accuracy in **assembly** tasks, particularly in electronics.
- **Compact Design**: SCARA robots are compact and can fit into smaller spaces, making them ideal for environments where space is limited.

Use Case:

- **Fanuc's SCARA robots** are used in electronics assembly to perform

soldering and **PCB assembly**. These robots perform high-precision operations, reducing human error and speeding up production cycles.

- **Case Study**: At **Samsung's smartphone assembly lines**, SCARA robots are used for high-precision tasks such as **screen installation**, **component placement**, and **inspection**. These robots work alongside human workers to automate tedious and repetitive operations.

Career Tip:

- **Skills Needed**: Knowledge of **SCARA robot programming** and **motion control**. Familiarity with **PLC integration** and **robot system design** will also be valuable.
- **Career Path**: Opportunities are abundant in industries such as **electronics manufacturing**, **consumer goods**, and **packaging**, where SCARA robots are used for fast, repetitive tasks.

Cartesian Robots

Description: Cartesian robots are characterized by **three linear actuators** that move along the **X, Y, and Z axes**, making them ideal for precise linear movements. They are straightforward in design and operation, which makes them an attractive option for applications where high repeatability and reliability are needed. Cartesian robots are typically used for **pick-and-place**, **3D printing**, and **automated testing**.

Key Features:

- **Simple Design**: Easy to build and program, making them suitable for basic, repetitive tasks.
- **Cost-Effective**: Generally less expensive than other types of robots.
- **Precise Movement**: Excellent for linear motions and handling small parts.

Use Case:

- **BMW** uses Cartesian robots in their **windshield installation** process at their plant in Leipzig. The robot precisely positions and installs the windshield, ensuring uniform pressure distribution and perfect fit every time.

Career Tip:

- **Skills Needed**: Learn **CAD** tools (like **AutoCAD** or **SolidWorks**) to design Cartesian robots. Understanding **motion control systems** and programming is crucial.
- **Career Path**: Companies that manufacture **automotive parts, consumer electronics**, or **medical devices** often seek professionals skilled in Cartesian robotics for tasks like assembly and material handling.

Delta Robots

Description: Delta robots are known for their **high-speed precision** and are used in applications that require quick movements and fine control, such as **sorting, picking**, and **packaging**. Their design involves three arms connected to a central platform, which allows them to move rapidly in multiple directions without compromising accuracy.

Key Features:

- **High Speed**: Ideal for applications where fast movements are required.
- **Compact Design**: Suitable for small-scale automation environments.
- **Precision**: Able to handle delicate items like food and pharmaceuticals.

Use Case:

- **Rethink Robotics' Sawyer** is a widely used delta robot in the **packaging and food industries**. For instance, it is used to pack **fresh fruits** into boxes at high speeds, significantly improving productivity while maintaining hygiene standards.

Career Tip:

- **Skills Needed**: **Robot design, high-speed motion control**, and **robot programming languages** like **URScript** for Universal Robots.

Career Path: Opportunities in industries such as **food processing, packaging**, and **pharmaceuticals** where high-speed precision is a priority.

4

Collaborative Robots (Cobots) and Safety

What Are Collaborative Robots?

Collaborative robots, commonly referred to as **cobots**, are robots specifically designed to work alongside human workers in shared workspaces. Unlike traditional industrial robots, which are typically enclosed within safety cages or barriers to prevent human interaction, cobots are engineered with advanced safety features to allow close interaction with humans. This enables a more flexible, efficient, and harmonious collaboration between humans and robots on the shop floor.

Cobots can perform a wide range of tasks that require high precision, such as **assembly**, **inspection**, **material handling**, and **packaging**. They are versatile tools that can assist workers by taking over repetitive or physically demanding tasks, thereby freeing up human workers to focus on more complex, strategic, or creative activities.

The growing popularity of cobots is driven by their ability to increase **productivity** and **efficiency** without the high safety and operational costs associated with traditional robotic systems.

Advantages of Cobots

Collaborative robots offer several benefits over traditional industrial robots and manual labor, making them an attractive option for many industries, from manufacturing to healthcare.

1. **Safety**
2.

- **Built-in Safety Features**: Cobots are designed with a range of **safety mechanisms** to ensure that they do not pose a risk to human workers. These features may include **force sensors** that detect when a robot comes into contact with a human and **automatically stop** or **reduce speed** to avoid injury. Additionally, cobots often have **soft-touch surfaces** and **rounded edges** to prevent sharp edges that could harm a human.
- **Collaborative Workspace**: Cobots operate without the need for **safety cages**, allowing them to work closely with humans. This reduces the physical barriers between human workers and automation, enabling more efficient and effective collaboration.

Flexibility

- **Reprogrammable and Adaptable**: Cobots are highly **flexible** in terms of the tasks they can perform. Unlike traditional robots that are typically custom-built for a single purpose, cobots can be easily reprogrammed or redeployed for different tasks. For instance, a cobot on an assembly line might initially be programmed for **screwing** parts together, but later can be reprogrammed to perform **inspection** or **packing** tasks without the need for significant retooling or downtime.
- **Ease of Integration**: Cobots can be easily integrated into existing workflows and can be used by non-expert operators. This ease of use helps companies of all sizes (especially small and medium-sized enterprises, SMEs) adopt robotic solutions without needing to hire a large, specialized workforce.

Cost-Efficiency

- **Lower Initial Investment**: Compared to traditional industrial robots, cobots are typically **more affordable**. They require less infrastructure, as they do not need to be placed in an isolated or restricted environment. Additionally, their **lower operational costs** and **ease of programming** mean that businesses can save on training and maintenance costs.

14

- **Scalability**: Because cobots are highly adaptable and easy to deploy, businesses can quickly scale automation efforts to meet demand, making them a more cost-effective option than traditional robotic solutions, especially for SMEs.

Use Case: Universal Robots (UR3)

Universal Robots (UR3) is one of the most popular cobots in use today. This small, lightweight, and flexible robot is particularly well-suited for **small and medium-sized enterprises (SMEs)** that require automation for tasks like **screwing, packing, inspection**, and **quality control**. The UR3 is able to work safely alongside human workers, sharing workspace without the need for safety barriers, making it an excellent choice for environments where space is limited.

- **Examples of Use**: Companies like **BMW** and **Volkswagen** have integrated **UR cobots** into their production lines. In these settings, the cobots perform tasks such as **screwing car parts, assembling components**, and even **inspecting parts** for quality, all while working side by side with human workers. This collaboration enhances overall productivity and ensures that workers can focus on more **complex** or **skilled tasks** that require human judgment.

Case Study: Tesla's Fremont Plant

At **Tesla's Fremont plant**, **Universal Robots cobots** play a significant role in improving the **efficiency** and **precision** of the assembly process. These cobots are deployed to assist human workers by performing **repetitive tasks**, such as **screwing** and **tightening bolts** during the engine assembly process.

Impact:

- **Enhanced Productivity**: By automating repetitive tasks, cobots reduce the time spent on manual operations, which speeds up production.

15

- **Reduction of Human Error**: The cobots' precision ensures that repetitive tasks are performed consistently without errors, reducing the likelihood of defects and improving the quality of the final product.
- **Safety**: Cobots work side-by-side with humans without the need for safety barriers, allowing workers to focus on higher-level tasks while cobots handle the more menial tasks. This collaboration helps reduce the physical strain on workers and minimizes the risks of workplace injuries.

The use of cobots in Tesla's plant showcases how automation can be seamlessly integrated into a fast-paced, high-quality manufacturing environment, enhancing both **efficiency** and **worker safety**.

Safety Considerations for Cobots

While cobots are inherently safer than traditional industrial robots, certain **safety considerations** must still be addressed to ensure a safe working environment. These include proper integration, setup, and ongoing monitoring to avoid any potential hazards.

Risk Assessment:

- Before deploying a cobot in a shared workspace, a **thorough risk assessment** should be conducted. This includes evaluating the nature of the tasks the cobot will perform, the level of interaction with human workers, and the physical environment. Identifying potential risks—such as the likelihood of the robot colliding with workers or performing an incorrect task—helps in ensuring safe operation.

Force Limiting:

- **Force sensors** are one of the most important safety features of cobots. These sensors can detect when the robot has come into contact with an object or human and automatically **stop or reduce its speed** to prevent injury. Force-limiting is crucial for ensuring that the cobot can work safely in close proximity to human operators, particularly in environments where the robot is performing tasks such as **assembly, welding,** or **painting.**

Safety Standards:

- Cobots are subject to various **safety standards,** including **ISO 10218,** which governs safety for industrial robots, and **ISO/TS 15066,** which specifically addresses the safety requirements for **collaborative robots.** Compliance with these standards ensures that cobots are designed to meet safety guidelines, such as limiting force, controlling speed, and enabling safe human-robot interactions.
- Additionally, companies deploying cobots should adhere to **local and international safety regulations** and implement **safety protocols** to maintain a secure working environment.

Ongoing Monitoring and Maintenance:

- Even though cobots are designed with safety features, regular **monitoring** and **maintenance** are essential to ensure their ongoing safe operation. Sensors, programming, and physical components must be periodically checked to ensure that they remain in good working condition and that no malfunctions could endanger workers.

Career Tip: Skills Needed for Working with Cobots

With the growing adoption of cobots, there are increasing opportunities for professionals with expertise in both **robotics** and **safety.** The following skills and knowledge areas are essential for those looking to enter or advance in the field of collaborative robotics:

- **Understanding Robot Safety Protocols:** Familiarity with safety standards like **ISO 10218** and **ISO/TS 15066** is crucial. A strong understanding of how to implement safety features and perform **risk assessments** in collaborative environments will set you apart.

- **Human-Robot Collaboration Design**: Expertise in designing systems where robots and humans can work together safely and efficiently is becoming increasingly important. This includes knowledge of **force sensors**, **programming** robots for collaborative tasks, and ensuring that the robots operate within safe limits.
- **Cobot Programming**: Cobots are often reprogrammed to handle different tasks. **Programming knowledge**—particularly in **robot programming languages** (like **URScript** for Universal Robots)—and the ability to adapt robots to different work environments will be in high demand.

Career Path:

- **Robot Safety Engineers**: Safety engineers specializing in collaborative robots will be highly sought after to help companies meet safety standards and maintain a safe working environment.
- **Robot Integration Specialists**: These professionals are responsible for integrating cobots into existing workflows. Their job involves ensuring that robots work seamlessly with human operators and other automation systems.
- **Robotics Technicians and Engineers**: As the demand for cobots increases, technicians and engineers with experience in **robot programming**, **maintenance**, and **system integration** will be needed to install, configure, and maintain cobots.

Conclusion

Collaborative robots (cobots) are transforming industries by enabling seamless human-robot collaboration, improving **efficiency**, and enhancing **workplace safety**. By providing **flexibility**, **cost-efficiency**, and **precision**, cobots are helping businesses across various sectors, from manufacturing to healthcare, to optimize their operations.

However, the integration of cobots requires careful attention to safety protocols, risk assessment, and compliance with international safety standards. As companies continue to adopt cobots, there will be increasing opportunities for professionals with specialized skills in robot safety, integration, and programming, ensuring that the collaborative robot ecosystem grows in a safe

5

Robot Sensors and Vision Systems

Overview:

Robots rely on **sensors** and **vision systems** to interact with their environment, perceive objects, and make decisions in real-time. These technologies enhance the capabilities of robots, enabling them to perform tasks such as object recognition, defect detection, and autonomous navigation.

Key Topics to Cover:

Types of Sensors in Robotics:

- **Proximity Sensors**: These sensors are used to detect the presence of objects without making physical contact. Common types include **capacitive**, **inductive**, and **ultrasonic sensors**, which are used in tasks like collision avoidance, object detection, and simple material handling.
- **Force Sensors**: These measure the amount of force being applied by a robot, helping it to interact more safely and effectively with objects or humans. Force sensors are critical for delicate assembly tasks, such as **precise insertion** or **screwing** operations.
- **Tactile Sensors**: Tactile sensors allow robots to feel and detect touch, much like a human sense of touch. These are used in tasks that require a robot to "feel" an object before acting, such as **grasping**, **cutting**, or **holding** fragile materials.

- **Infrared (IR) Sensors**: These sensors use infrared light to detect nearby objects or measure distances. They are widely used in **navigation systems** for robots, helping them to avoid obstacles or measure distance in real-time.

Machine Vision Systems:

- **2D Vision**: Traditional camera-based vision systems that capture images in two dimensions. 2D vision is often used for **quality inspection, barcode scanning**, and **object identification**.
- **3D Vision**: Advanced systems that provide depth information, allowing robots to perceive objects in three dimensions. This is particularly important for tasks like **robotic pick-and-place, assembly**, and **defect detection** where depth perception is crucial.
- **Depth Sensing**: Technologies like **LIDAR (Light Detection and Ranging)** and **structured light** help robots measure the distance to objects in their environment, enhancing navigation, obstacle avoidance, and part handling.
- **Stereo Vision**: This involves two or more cameras working in tandem to create a depth map of the environment. It is particularly useful for robots involved in **3D scanning, inspection**, and **mapping**.

Artificial Vision and AI:

- **Deep Learning for Object Recognition**: Using **convolutional neural networks (CNNs)**, robots can learn to recognize objects, faces, and even defects in complex environments. For instance, deep learning algorithms are used in **automated quality control systems** to inspect items in production.
- **Image Segmentation**: AI-powered vision systems can segment images into different regions or objects, helping robots to distinguish between parts and decide which actions to take. This technique is used in **robotic assembly** and **sorting** operations.

21

- **Adaptive Vision Systems**: These systems adjust to changing lighting conditions, varying shapes, and unexpected obstructions, allowing robots to work in more dynamic and unpredictable environments, like **warehouses** or **construction sites**.

Case Studies:

- **Cognex Vision Systems in KUKA Robots**:
- KUKA robots equipped with **Cognex vision systems** are used in **automotive manufacturing** to detect defects in parts. The robots perform visual inspection of **car doors**, checking for issues such as scratches, dents, and misalignments. This automated visual inspection improves accuracy and reduces errors in the manufacturing process.

- **ABB's Vision System in Food Packaging**:
- ABB's robots use vision systems to identify and pick food products from conveyor belts. For example, **Nestlé** employs ABB robots with vision sensors in their packaging lines to select and package items like chocolate bars. The vision system allows robots to differentiate between different products and handle them delicately, which ensures that fragile items aren't damaged during packaging.

Career Tip:

Understanding **image processing**, **3D vision systems**, and **sensor integration** is crucial for anyone looking to specialize in robotics, particularly in **quality control**, **inspection**, and **autonomous systems**. Gaining expertise in platforms like **OpenCV** and **ROS (Robot Operating System)** can boost your employ ability.

6

Human-Robot Interaction (HRI)

Overview:

As robots become more integrated into workplaces, understanding **Human-Robot Interaction (HRI)** is essential. This section delves into how robots can collaborate with humans in a shared environment, ensuring safety, efficiency, and user-friendliness.

Key Topics to Cover:

Fundamentals of HRI:

- **Communication Protocols**: Robots and humans need a common communication language. This can involve **visual cues** (like lights or screens), **auditory signals** (sound alerts or spoken commands), or even **gestures** (recognized by cameras or sensors).
- **Feedback Loops**: Robots often rely on feedback loops to interact effectively with humans. For example, if a robot is programmed to **pick and place** an item, it might use a **haptic feedback** system to notify a human operator if an action has been completed successfully or if assistance is required.
- **Trust and Collaboration**: For robots to work alongside humans effectively, there needs to be **mutual trust**. This involves the robot demonstrating its reliability and safety in the workplace through pre-

dictable behavior.

User Interfaces:

- **Touchscreen Interfaces**: Many robots now feature intuitive touchscreen interfaces that allow workers to control robot movements, adjust settings, and monitor performance in real-time. These interfaces are often seen in **automated machines** or **cobots** used in light assembly lines.
- **Voice Commands**: With the integration of natural language processing (NLP) technologies, robots can respond to spoken commands. This is increasingly used in service robots, where **voice interaction** is critical for accessibility and ease of use.
- **Gesture Recognition**: Robots equipped with cameras and vision systems can recognize hand gestures, allowing operators to control robots via gestures. This is particularly useful in scenarios where the operator is unable to use a traditional controller or screen, such as in **clean room environments** or **assembly lines**.

Safety and Comfort:

- **Collision Detection and Avoidance**: Robots use sensors (e.g., **force sensors** or **LIDAR**) to detect when they are approaching a human or another object, enabling them to stop or alter their movement to avoid accidents.
- **Speed and Force Control**: Many robots are programmed to operate at lower speeds when near humans, and force control algorithms help ensure that robots do not apply excessive force when interacting with people or fragile objects.
- **Safety Standards**: Robots working in human environments must comply with various safety standards such as **ISO 10218** (for industrial robots) and **ISO/TS 15066** (for collaborative robots), which outline safety measures to minimize risk during human-robot interaction.

Case Studies:

- **BMW Spartanburg Plant (Cobots):**
- BMW employs **collaborative robots (cobots)** alongside human workers in the **Spartanburg** plant in South Carolina. The robots assist in assembly tasks, such as part insertion and welding, while human workers focus on tasks that require complex decision-making. The robots are programmed to stop immediately if they detect an unexpected interaction with a human, ensuring **worker safety** and **task efficiency**.

- **Ford's Use of Cobots in Car Assembly**:
- Ford Motor Company has integrated cobots into their car assembly lines in **Detroit**. These cobots work alongside workers to insert parts and fasten screws, enhancing **assembly line efficiency** while reducing physical strain on workers. The collaborative setup also reduces the likelihood of errors, as the cobots perform repetitive tasks with precision, and human workers focus on more complex tasks.

Career Tip:

For those interested in HRI, learning how to design **user-friendly interfaces**, ensuring **ergonomics** in robot-human collaboration, and understanding **human factors engineering** will be key. Being knowledgeable about safety standards like **ISO/TS 15066** can make you highly valuable in industries adopting **cobots**.

7

Industrial Robot Maintenance and Troubleshooting

Overview:

To ensure maximum uptime, industrial robots require regular maintenance and effective troubleshooting when issues arise. This section covers maintenance strategies, including **preventive**, **predictive**, and **corrective** approaches, and offers insights into diagnosing and resolving common robot issues.

Key Topics to Cover:

Routine Maintenance:

- **Cleaning**: Regular cleaning of robot parts, especially sensors and actuators, ensures optimal performance. Dust, dirt, and grease can hinder the movement of robotic arms or impair sensors, so keeping robots clean is essential.
- **Lubrication**: Regular lubrication of moving parts such as joints, actuators, and gears helps prevent wear and tear, reduces friction, and extends the life of robotic components.
- **Calibration**: Periodically checking and recalibrating the robot's sensors and actuators ensures that it continues to perform tasks with high

accuracy. This is especially important for robots used in **precision manufacturing** or **quality control** tasks.

Predictive Maintenance:

- **IoT Sensors and Data Analytics**: Robots are increasingly equipped with **IoT sensors** that collect data on motor temperature, vibration, and power consumption. Using **big data analytics**, operators can predict when parts are likely to fail and schedule maintenance before a breakdown occurs.
- **Machine Learning for Fault Prediction**: **Machine learning algorithms** can process vast amounts of sensor data to detect patterns that indicate potential failures, such as **increased temperature** in a motor or **irregular vibrations** in a joint.
- **Remote Monitoring**: Many companies now offer remote monitoring services, where specialists can track robot performance in real-time. This is particularly useful for robots operating in remote or hazardous environments, such as offshore oil rigs or underground mining operations.

Troubleshooting Common Robot Failures:

- **Loss of Motion**: One of the most common issues is the loss of motion in robotic arms or joints. This could be due to issues with the **servo motors**, **gearboxes**, or the **controller**. A diagnostic check is required to pinpoint the issue.
- **Sensor Failures**: If a robot relies heavily on sensors for navigation or interaction, sensor malfunctions can cause errors in behavior. For example, **proximity sensors** may stop detecting objects, or **vision systems** may provide incorrect readings. Troubleshooting involves checking wiring connections, recalibrating sensors, or replacing faulty units.
- **Controller Malfunctions**: A malfunction in the **controller** or the **software** can prevent robots from performing tasks as intended. Diagnosing

this issue typically involves rebooting systems, checking for software updates, or recalibrating control algorithms.

Case Studies:

- **Siemens Predictive Maintenance in Automotive Manufacturing**:
- Siemens provides predictive maintenance solutions using **IoT sensors** and **machine learning** to monitor robots in **automotive manufacturing plants**. By constantly collecting data on robot performance, Siemens can predict when a failure is likely to occur, enabling the manufacturer to perform repairs proactively, reducing **downtime** and **costs**.
-
- **KUKA Maintenance at Ford Motor Company**:
- Ford employs KUKA robots in its assembly lines. By using **KUKA's Smart Maintenance** system, the company monitors robot components in real-time. This predictive maintenance system helps identify wear and tear on robot parts before they cause a breakdown, minimizing costly unplanned downtime and improving the overall **reliability** of the robots.

Career Tip:

Professionals skilled in **robot diagnostics**, **sensor integration**, and **data analysis for predictive maintenance** will be in high demand, especially in industries like automotive and **aerospace**, where up time is critical. Familiarity with **machine learning** and **AI-based systems** will also be advantageous.

8

Robot Simulation and Virtual Commissioning

Overview:

Simulation software allows engineers to model robot behavior before actual deployment, helping to optimize robot paths, validate system designs, and reduce commissioning time. This section explains **robot simulation** and the role of **virtual commissioning** in streamlining robot integration into production lines.

Key Topics to Cover:

Robot Simulation Software:

- **Offline Programming**: **Offline programming tools** such as **RoboDK** and **RobotStudio** allow engineers to program robots in a virtual environment before sending the instructions to the physical robot. This approach reduces downtime and improves efficiency.
- **Robot Path Optimization**: Simulation software is used to optimize the robot's path, minimizing cycle times and improving production efficiency. These tools allow engineers to test and refine movements without wasting materials or resources.
- **Collision Detection in Simulation**: Before deploying robots in a real-

world setting, simulations can check for potential **collisions** with the environment or other robots. This is crucial for preventing damage to machinery or injury to workers during actual deployment.

Virtual Commissioning:

- **Digital Twin Technology**: **Digital twins** are virtual replicas of physical robots and production lines. These replicas are used to simulate real-world scenarios, making it easier to test robot performance in various conditions and workflows without disrupting the actual production process.
- **Integration Testing**: Virtual commissioning enables engineers to test how robots will integrate with other parts of the production line, such as **conveyor systems**, **sensors**, and **PLC controllers**. This ensures smooth operations before robots are physically installed.
- **Risk Assessment**: Virtual commissioning can identify potential risks in the production environment, such as **software conflicts** or **hardware malfunctions**, helping engineers to troubleshoot and resolve these issues before going live.

Benefits of Simulation: Reduced errors, faster setup, and early troubleshooting.

Case Studies:

- **ABB RobotStudio at Ford**:
- Ford uses **ABB's RobotStudio** to simulate robot movements before they are physically deployed on the assembly line. This allows Ford to test different configurations and make necessary adjustments before installation, reducing **downtime** and **rework** during actual production.

- **Volkswagen Virtual Commissioning**:
- **Volkswagen** uses **virtual commissioning** to simulate their entire robotic assembly process in **their Wolfsburg plant**. By creating a digital twin of the production line, they can test robot actions, workflow integration, and safety protocols in a virtual environment, reducing the time it takes to deploy robots on the factory floor.

Career Tip:

Gaining proficiency in simulation tools like **RobotStudio** or **RoboDK** is essential for engineers working in automation. Learning how to integrate **digital twins** and **offline programming** into real-world robotic systems can give you a significant edge in industries that require **high precision** and **efficiency**.

9

Autonomous Mobile Robots (AMRs)

Overview:

Autonomous Mobile Robots (AMRs) are increasingly used for material transport, navigation, and logistics. These robots can navigate autonomously in dynamic environments, enabling efficient material handling and distribution in factories and warehouses.

Key Topics to Cover:

MR Design and Navigation:

- **LIDAR and SLAM**: AMRs use **LIDAR** (Light Detection and Ranging) to create a detailed map of their surroundings and employ **SLAM (Simultaneous Localization and Mapping)** to navigate complex environments autonomously. These technologies enable AMRs to avoid obstacles and plan efficient routes through warehouses or factories.
- **Path Planning Algorithms**: AMRs use advanced algorithms to calculate the most efficient path between two points while avoiding obstacles. These algorithms can adapt to changing environments, such as dynamically moving obstacles or shifting layouts in a warehouse.
- **Sensor Fusion**: Combining data from multiple sensors, including **LIDAR, cameras, ultrasonic sensors**, and **GPS**, allows AMRs to accurately map their surroundings and make informed decisions in real-

time.

Applications in Logistics:

- **Material Handling**: AMRs are increasingly used in **warehouses** to move materials from one location to another, reducing the need for manual labor. They can transport goods from storage areas to picking stations, assembly lines, or shipping docks.
- **Goods-to-Person Systems**: In this system, AMRs transport products to human workers who pick and pack items, improving productivity by reducing the time workers spend walking around the warehouse. Companies like **Ocado** and **Zara** have implemented this technology in their **fulfillment centers**.
- **Inventory Management**: AMRs are also used for real-time inventory management. Equipped with RFID or barcode scanners, they can automatically count and track inventory levels in warehouses, reducing human errors and enhancing stock accuracy.

Integration with Other Systems:

- **Warehouse Management Systems (WMS)**: AMRs are often integrated with **WMS** to synchronize material transport with **inventory control**. For instance, an AMR may pick up an order from a designated location and deliver it to a specific worker based on **real-time orders**.
- **Robotic Process Automation (RPA)**: AMRs are also integrated with **RPA** systems to optimize **logistical workflows**, such as loading and unloading, stock replenishment, and item sorting. This integration creates seamless, end-to-end automation in logistics.

Case Studies:

- **Amazon Robotics (Kiva Systems)**:

- Amazon employs **Kiva robots** to transport inventory within its massive warehouses. These robots use a combination of **LIDAR** and **SLAM** technologies to autonomously navigate the warehouse, bringing shelves to human workers for picking and packing. This significantly reduces the time spent walking around the warehouse and boosts efficiency.

- **BMW's Use of AMRs in Logistics**:
- BMW uses **AMRs** to autonomously transport parts between different production areas within its factories. The robots are integrated into the **factory's WMS** and help reduce human labor costs and improve **inventory accuracy** by providing real-time data on part locations.

Career Tip:

Specializing in **robot navigation algorithms, path planning**, and **integration of AMRs** with **warehouse management systems** can make you a sought-after expert in industries like **logistics, retail**, and **e-commerce**.

10

Ethics and Social Impact of Robotics and Automation

Overview:

As automation becomes more widespread, its ethical implications grow. This section discusses potential social and economic impacts, such as **job displacement**, **autonomous decision-making**, and the role of **privacy** in robotic systems.

Job Displacement vs. Job Creation: How Automation May Replace Certain Jobs but Also Create New Roles in Development, Maintenance, and Integration

The Impact of Automation on Employment

One of the most significant debates surrounding the rise of robotics and automation is the potential for **job displacement**. While it is true that automation technologies, including robots, AI, and machine learning, have the potential to **replace certain jobs**, they also create new opportunities, particularly in **robot development**, **maintenance**, **integration**, and **AI programming**.

Job Displacement

As robots and AI become more capable, they are increasingly able to perform tasks traditionally done by humans. Some jobs are more susceptible to automation than others:

- **Repetitive and Manual Jobs**: Occupations that require repetitive tasks, like **assembly line workers**, **warehouse staff**, and **customer service representatives**, are highly vulnerable. Robots can perform these tasks faster, more accurately, and without fatigue. For example, in **manufacturing**, robots can handle **material sorting**, **welding**, and **painting**, potentially displacing human workers.
- **Dangerous Jobs**: Jobs that involve hazardous conditions, such as **mining**, **construction**, or **handling toxic materials**, are also at risk. Autonomous robots, drones, and exoskeletons can perform tasks in hazardous environments, reducing human exposure to dangerous situations.
- **Low-Skilled Roles**: **Cashiers**, **clerks**, and **delivery drivers** are examples of low-skilled roles that can be replaced by automation. For instance, self-checkout kiosks in retail stores are already replacing human cashiers, and self-driving vehicles are set to replace truck drivers and couriers.

Job Creation

On the other hand, automation and robotics can also generate a wide range of new roles that require different skill sets. As robots take over repetitive, dangerous, or manual tasks, there is a growing demand for professionals in more complex areas:

- **Robot Development and Engineering**: The demand for **robotics engineers**, **AI specialists**, and **mechanical engineers** will continue to grow. Professionals in these fields design, build, and optimize robots, often requiring expertise in **machine learning**, **sensor integration**,

vision systems, and **autonomous decision-making algorithms**.

- **Maintenance and Repair**: While robots can perform many tasks autonomously, they still require regular maintenance and repair. **Robot technicians**, **maintenance engineers**, and **service engineers** will be needed to ensure that the robots operate efficiently and safely. This includes maintaining the robots' physical components, sensors, and software systems.

- **System Integration**: The integration of robots into existing manufacturing or service systems requires experts in **robot integration** and **automation systems**. These professionals ensure that robots are properly integrated into workflows, work collaboratively with human operators, and function seamlessly within larger technological ecosystems.

- **Data Scientists and AI Developers**: With the rise of **AI-driven robotics**, professionals who specialize in **data science**, **machine learning**, and **deep learning** are in high demand. These experts work on algorithms that allow robots to make autonomous decisions, process data from sensors, and learn from experience.

- **Human-Robot Interaction (HRI) Experts**: As robots become more integrated into everyday environments, particularly in **healthcare** and **customer service**, there is a growing need for **human-robot interaction** specialists. These professionals focus on designing robots that can effectively and safely interact with humans, ensuring that robots are both helpful and intuitive.

Conclusion

While automation may displace some traditional jobs, it is also creating new roles that require specialized skills. The key to minimizing the negative impacts of job displacement is **up skilling** and **re skilling** workers to take on new roles in developing, maintaining, and integrating automation systems. As industries adapt to automation, there will be an increasing need for a skilled workforce to manage and advance the technology.

11

Robotic Programming and Integration with PLCs

The Basics of Robotic Programming

Robotic programming involves creating the commands that control the robot's actions. This can be done through different methods such as **teach pendants**, **graphical programming**, and **offline programming**.

Teach Pendant Programming

In this method, operators physically move the robot arm and record the positions via a **teach pendant** (a hand-held device). This approach is simple and effective for relatively simple, repetitive tasks.

Case Study:

- **Toyota** uses teach pendant programming for basic tasks like **welding** and **assembly** in its **Toyota Production System (TPS)**. Operators manually guide the robots to program their motions, saving time in setup and minimizing errors.

Career Tip:

- **Skills Needed**: Learning to operate **teach pendants** (common in **Fanuc** and **KUKA** robots) is key. Knowledge of **basic robot programming** and **motion control** can provide a solid foundation for further specialization.

Graphical Programming

Graphical programming allows users to program robots using visual interfaces instead of writing code. This is especially useful for beginners who may not be familiar with programming languages but need to quickly create programs.

Case Study:

- **ABB's RobotStudio** is a graphical programming software that enables users to simulate robot actions before deployment. This helps companies like **Ford** and **GM** to optimize robotic operations without disrupting production.

Career Tip:

- **Skills Needed**: Familiarity with **RobotStudio**, **Vuforia**, or similar programming environments will make you proficient in **robot simulation**. Understanding how to set up simulations can help optimize workflows in manufacturing and testing environments.

PLC Integration in Robotics

PLCs (Programmable Logic Controllers) are used to control and automate machines and processes. Integrating PLCs with robots is essential for coordinating robot actions with other systems, such as conveyors, sensors, and actuators.

Key Concepts of PLC Integration:

- **Communication**: PLCs communicate with robots to send and receive data about the process state, trigger actions, and synchronize different machine functions.

- **I/O Control**: The PLC manages input and output devices that robots interact with, such as **sensors**, **motors**, and **grippers**.

Use Case:

- **Boeing** uses **Siemens PLCs** to control the automation systems in its **aircraft assembly lines**, where robots are integrated with other machinery for tasks like **assembly**, **inspection**, and **painting**. The PLC ensures that robots perform tasks in synchronization with other equipment.

Career Tip:

- **Skills Needed**: Knowledge of **Siemens**, **Allen-Bradley**, and **Omron** PLCs is crucial for integrating robots into automated systems. Also, understanding **industrial communication protocols** (e.g., **Modbus**, **EtherCAT**) will enhance your integration skills.

Career Path: The manufacturing, aerospace, and automotive sectors are see

12

Autonomous Decision Making

Ethical Issues Around Robots Making Decisions in Critical Areas Like Healthcare, Military, and Customer Service

The Rise of Autonomous Decision-Making

Autonomous robots are increasingly capable of making decisions without human input, especially in areas like **healthcare**, the **military**, and **customer service**. These systems leverage **artificial intelligence** (AI), **machine learning**, and **big data** to make real-time decisions. While these technologies can enhance efficiency, safety, and precision, they also raise several **ethical concerns**.

Ethical Issues in Autonomous Decision Making

Healthcare and Medical Decision-Making

- **Accuracy vs. Accountability**: In healthcare, robots are being deployed
  to assist in diagnostic decision-making, **surgical procedures**, and even
  patient care. Autonomous systems can analyze medical images and data
  with high precision. However, when it comes to critical decisions—such

as diagnosing a disease or determining the best treatment plan—there is a risk that AI could make errors. **Who is accountable** if a machine makes an incorrect decision, leading to patient harm?

- **Bias and Fairness**: AI-driven medical systems often rely on large datasets to train their algorithms. If these datasets are **biased** (e.g., underrepresentation of certain demographic groups), the system may develop biased decision-making, leading to poorer outcomes for certain groups of patients. Ensuring **fairness** and eliminating bias in AI models is a major ethical challenge in healthcare.

- **Informed Consent**: In some cases, AI may recommend treatments or procedures that patients are not fully aware of, raising concerns about **informed consent**. Patients may not fully understand how an autonomous system arrived at a recommendation or treatment plan, which could undermine their trust in the healthcare system.

- **Patient Privacy**: Autonomous robots in healthcare often rely on **sensitive patient data** to make decisions. The privacy and security of this data are paramount, especially given the risks of data breaches. How autonomous systems handle this data and whether patients' privacy is adequately protected are major ethical concerns.

Military and Defense

- **Autonomous Weapons**: One of the most contentious issues in autonomous decision-making is the development of **autonomous weapons systems** (AWS). These systems are designed to carry out military tasks without human intervention, such as targeting and engaging enemies. Ethical concerns arise when robots make life-and-death decisions without human oversight. For example, what happens if an autonomous drone mistakes a civilian for an enemy combatant? The **accountability** for such decisions becomes blurred.

- **War Ethics and Human Oversight**: Many argue that the **human element** should remain in control of decisions related to life-or-death situations. While robots can help improve efficiency and minimize risks to human soldiers, the complete removal of human judgment in warfare raises deep concerns about accountability and responsibility.

- **Potential for Misuse**: The deployment of autonomous systems in warfare could lead to a **proliferation of autonomous weapons** in the wrong hands, such as terrorist organizations or rogue states, raising questions about **global security**.

Customer Service and Personal Assistants

- **Decision-Making Without Empathy**: Autonomous systems in **customer service** (e.g., chatbots, virtual assistants, and self-service kiosks) can make decisions based on patterns and algorithms, but they lack **empathy**. In sensitive situations, such as dealing with complaints or resolving conflicts, an automated system might not provide the nuanced response that a human would. This can result in poor customer experiences and even escalate conflicts.
- **Loss of Jobs**: AI-driven customer service systems can lead to the displacement of human workers, raising ethical concerns about **job loss** and the effects of **automation** on livelihoods. Additionally, there are concerns about the **dehumanization** of customer service, where customers may feel frustrated by the lack of personal interaction.
- **Privacy and Data Usage**: Many autonomous customer service systems collect vast amounts of personal data to improve their services. Ethical issues arise when users are unaware of how their data is being used or when this data is misused by the companies behind the AI systems.

Conclusion

The ethical concerns surrounding autonomous decision-making in critical areas are complex and require careful consideration. Balancing the benefits of automation—such as improved efficiency and reduced human error—with the potential risks and ethical dilemmas is crucial. It is essential to establish **clear regulations** and **oversight mechanisms** to ensure that autonomous systems act in a way that is ethical, transparent, and accountable.

13

Privacy and Surveillance

Concerns Over Robots with Cameras and Sensors Being Used for Surveillance in Public Spaces

The Rise of Surveillance Robots

With the increasing integration of **robotics** and **AI**, robots equipped with **cameras, sensors,** and **data-gathering capabilities** are becoming more common in public spaces. These robots are deployed for a variety of tasks, including **security monitoring, crowd management,** and **environmental scanning**. While these robots can enhance public safety and efficiency, they also raise significant concerns about **privacy** and **surveillance**.

Key Privacy Concerns

Unwarranted Surveillance:

- **Constant Monitoring:** Surveillance robots, especially in **public spaces**, such as shopping malls, airports, and streets, often operate **continuously**, collecting data on individuals' movements and behaviors. The issue arises when individuals are unaware they are being monitored, which can feel like an **invasion of privacy**. People may feel uncomfortable or unsafe

47

knowing they are constantly being observed by autonomous systems, which could have a chilling effect on **free expression** and **behavior**.

- **Lack of Consent**: In many instances, individuals are not asked for their **consent** before being monitored by surveillance robots. Unlike human surveillance officers who might require specific authorization or oversight, robots can record data without explicit consent, raising concerns about **data ownership** and **personal rights**.

Data Privacy and Security:

- **Data Collection and Storage**: Surveillance robots often collect massive amounts of personal data, including **facial images**, **voice recordings**, and **movement patterns**. This data can be used for various purposes, from identifying criminals to profiling individuals. However, this raises questions about how long the data is stored, who has access to it, and whether it can be used for purposes that the individual did not intend or approve of.

- **Data Breaches and Cybersecurity**: The sensitive data gathered by surveillance robots makes them a target for **cyberattacks**. If a breach occurs, personal information, including **biometric data** (e.g., facial recognition), could be compromised, leading to privacy violations, identity theft, or misuse of information.

Social Control and Behavior Manipulation:

- **Behavioral Manipulation**: When people are aware that they are being surveilled by robots, their behavior may change, often referred to as the **Panopticon effect**. This can result in individuals acting in more **conformist** ways, as they know their actions are being observed. While this may deter criminal activity, it could also restrict personal freedoms and **autonomy**, particularly in societies where surveillance is pervasive.

Discrimination and Profiling:

- **Bias in Surveillance Algorithms**: Robots equipped with **AI-driven facial recognition systems** can sometimes exhibit bias, particularly if the data sets used to train the system are not diverse enough. This can lead to **discriminatory practices**, such as falsely identifying individuals based on race, gender, or ethnicity. In highly surveilled areas, such biased systems could disproportionately target certain groups of people, leading to **racial profiling** or **unjust detention**.

Conclusion

While surveillance robots can improve public safety and operational efficiency, the ethical implications of their use in public spaces are profound. A careful balance must be struck between the **benefits** of using such technologies for security and the **risks** associated with eroding personal privacy. Governments and organizations deploying these systems must establish **clear guidelines, transparency,** and **regulations** to protect individuals' privacy and ensure that the use of surveillance robots is both ethical and responsible.

Case Studies:

- **Boston Dynamics and Surveillance Robots**:
- Boston Dynamics' **Spot robot**, equipped with cameras, is used in industries like construction and utilities to inspect hazardous areas. However, the robot has sparked debates over **privacy**, as it can also be used for **surveillance** purposes in public spaces. This raises ethical questions about the balance between innovation and **personal privacy**.

- **Foxconn and Job Displacement**:
- Foxconn has integrated **robots** into its production lines in China, replacing human workers for repetitive tasks like **welding** and **assembly**.

While the company claims that the robots improve productivity, it has also led to discussions on how automation is contributing to **job displacement** and the potential for **socioeconomic inequality**.

Career Tip:

Professionals with expertise in **robotics ethics**, **AI governance**, and **human-centric design** are increasingly needed to ensure that robots are integrated into society in a responsible, **fair**, and **equitable** manner.

14

Leading Companies Offering Robotics

The field of industrial robotics is growing rapidly, with several companies pioneering new technologies, solutions, and applications across diverse sectors. Understanding these industry leaders is essential for anyone looking to pursue a career or build expertise in robotics.

1. ABB Robotics

Major Offerings:

- **Industrial Robots**: ABB provides a wide range of robots for industrial automation, including articulated robots, SCARA robots, and delta robots. Their robots are used in a variety of applications such as **welding**, **assembly**, **material handling**, and **packaging**.
- **Collaborative Robots (Cobots)**: ABB's **YuMi** is a dual-arm collaborative robot designed for small parts assembly in electronics and consumer goods.
- **Robot Software & Controls**: ABB's **RobotStudio** is a leading simulation and offline programming software used to design, program, and optimize robots without interrupting production.
- **Robotic Solutions for Healthcare**: ABB has also developed robotic solutions for the **medical** and **pharmaceutical industries**, particularly in **automated drug manufacturing** and **robot-assisted surgeries**.

Key Strengths:

- **Global Reach**: ABB operates in over 100 countries and serves a wide array of industries from automotive to consumer electronics.
- **Innovation in Robotics**: ABB's robots are among the most flexible in the industry, with the ability to be reprogrammed for various tasks. They continue to innovate in the fields of **AI**, **machine learning**, and **robot autonomy**.
- **Comprehensive Services**: In addition to robots, ABB offers a full suite of services, including **robot programming**, **simulation**, and **preventive maintenance**, providing end-to-end automation solutions.

Leading Customers:

- **BMW**: ABB robots are used in BMW's manufacturing plants for welding, assembly, and handling components.
- **Tesla**: ABB robots are used in **Tesla's Gigafactories** for automation in battery production and assembly lines.
- **Amazon**: ABB collaborates with Amazon in warehouse automation, where its robots help with material handling and picking.

Job Prospects:

- ABB is a major employer in the field of robotics, offering job opportunities in **robot programming**, **system integration**, **R&D**, and **field service**. Positions like **robotics engineer**, **automation specialist**, and **robotics software developer** are in high demand.
- ABB also offers internships and graduate programs in various fields of robotics, making it a great entry point for new graduates.

2. KUKA Robotics
Major Offerings:

- **Industrial Robots**: KUKA offers a range of industrial robots, including the **KR AGILUS** for precision tasks, **KR QUANTEC** for heavy-duty tasks, and the **KR IONTEC** series for versatile production lines.
- **Collaborative Robots (Cobots)**: KUKA's **LBR iiwa** is a lightweight robot designed for human-robot collaboration, used in applications such as **assembly, quality control**, and **packaging**.
- **Robotic Systems for Automation**: KUKA provides end-to-end robotic systems, including **robot arms, grippers**, and **vision systems**, integrated into complete automation solutions for industries such as automotive, electronics, and metalworking.
- **Robotics Software**: KUKA's **KUKA.Sim** is used for robot simulation and offline programming, allowing for efficient robot deployment and optimization.

Key Strengths:

- **Industry Expertise**: KUKA has a long history in the robotics field, with a strong presence in **automotive manufacturing**, particularly in **welding, painting**, and **assembly**.
- **Flexibility and Customization**: KUKA robots are known for their adaptability and are highly customizable to fit the needs of various industries.
- **High Precision and Durability**: KUKA robots are designed to handle high-precision tasks, making them ideal for industries like aerospace and electronics manufacturing.

Leading Customers:

- **Volkswagen**: KUKA robots are widely used in **Volkswagen's** automotive manufacturing plants, including in **welding** and **assembly** lines.
- **Tesla**: KUKA has collaborated with **Tesla** for robotic automation in the electric vehicle manufacturing process, especially for **battery production** and **vehicle assembly**.

- **Daimler**: KUKA provides robotic solutions for **Daimler's** automotive assembly lines, particularly in **welding** and **painting**.

Job Prospects:

- KUKA offers careers in **robotics engineering, automation systems integration**, and **robot programming**. Positions like **control engineer, robotics software developer**, and **technical sales engineer** are key areas where KUKA is hiring.
- KUKA also offers opportunities in **research and development (R&D)**, focusing on cutting-edge automation technologies, and positions in **customer service** and **technical support** for global clients.

3. FANUC Corporation
   Major Offerings:

- **Industrial Robots**: FANUC offers a range of robots, from **articulated robots** like the **M-20iA** to **delta robots** like the **M-1iA**. Their robots are used in **assembly, material handling, welding**, and **painting**.
- **Collaborative Robots (Cobots)**: FANUC's **CR Series** cobots are designed for easy human-robot collaboration, helping workers with tasks like **parts feeding, assembly**, and **quality inspection**.
- **Robot Controllers and Software**: FANUC provides powerful controllers such as the **R-30iB** and software for programming and controlling robots, with integrated **AI** and **machine learning** capabilities.
- **Robotic Welding Solutions**: FANUC's robotic welding solutions, such as the **ARC Mate** series, are widely used in the automotive and manufacturing industries.

Key Strengths:

- **Global Market Leader**: FANUC is one of the largest and most well-

54

known robotics companies worldwide, with over **400,000 robots** installed globally.

- **Reliability and Durability**: FANUC robots are highly reliable and designed for long-lasting performance in high-demand manufacturing environments.
- **Advanced Robotics Solutions**: FANUC continues to innovate in robotics, focusing on incorporating **AI, vision systems**, and **machine learning** into their products to improve performance and adaptability.

Leading Customers:

- **Honda**: FANUC robots are widely used in **Honda's** automotive manufacturing plants, especially for **welding, assembly**, and **material handling**.
- **General Motors**: GM utilizes FANUC robots in their **automotive assembly lines** for tasks such as **spot welding** and **robotic painting**.
- **Samsung**: FANUC collaborates with **Samsung** in **electronics manufacturing**, where its robots are used for **pick and place, inspection**, and **packaging** operations.

Job Prospects:

- FANUC provides opportunities in **robotics engineering, AI and machine learning** development, and **robot maintenance**. Positions like **robotics integration engineer, software developer**, and **customer support engineer** are common job openings.
- FANUC also hires for **technical sales** roles to support the adoption of robotic solutions by new customers in industries ranging from automotive to electronics.

4. Universal Robots
   Major Offerings:

- **Collaborative Robots (Cobots)**: Universal Robots specializes in **cobots**, with models like the **UR3e**, **UR5e**, and **UR10e** designed to perform tasks such as **assembly**, **packaging**, **inspection**, and **quality control** in close collaboration with human workers.

- **Robot Arms**: These flexible, lightweight robots can be programmed for various applications in industries such as electronics, automotive, and consumer goods.
- **End Effectors and Software**: Universal Robots also offers a range of **end effectors** (grippers, tools) and an easy-to-use **robot programming software** that allows non-technical users to deploy robots on the production floor without prior robotics experience.

Key Strengths:

- **Ease of Use**: One of Universal Robots' key strengths is the user-friendly design of their robots. They are designed to be easily programmed and integrated, even by users with little or no prior robotics experience.
- **Flexible Automation Solutions**: Their cobots can be deployed in a variety of industries and adapted to different types of tasks, making them highly versatile.
- **Strong Partner Ecosystem**: Universal Robots has built a robust ecosystem of **partners** who provide specialized accessories, software, and integration services to enhance the capabilities of their robots.

Leading Customers:

- **Ford**: Universal Robots' cobots have been deployed in **Ford's** production facilities for tasks such as **assembly** and **quality control**.
- **L'Oréal**: L'Oréal uses Universal Robots for **packaging** and **product inspection** at its manufacturing plants.
- **Coca-Cola**: Coca-Cola uses Universal Robots in **material handling** and **palletizing** processes at its bottling plants.

Job Prospects:

- Universal Robots offers career opportunities in **robotics integration, software development, product design**, and **sales engineering**. They seek professionals with expertise in **robot programming, cobot deployment**, and **technical support**.
- With the increasing adoption of cobots in small to medium-sized enterprises (SMEs), there are growing opportunities in **cobot integration consulting** and **training** roles for individuals looking to specialize in collaborative robotics.

5. Boston Dynamics
Major Offerings:

- **Mobile Robots**: Boston Dynamics' **Spot** robot is a highly agile, four-legged robot designed for tasks such as **inspection, surveying**, and **logistics** in difficult-to-reach environments.
- **Robot Systems for Inspection**: Spot has been equipped with advanced sensors and cameras to perform autonomous inspections in industries such as **construction, energy**, and **mining**.
- **Atlas**: **Atlas** is a humanoid robot designed for high-mobility tasks and complex environments, capable of performing tasks such as **jumping, running**, and **backflips**, and has been used for demonstrations in industrial and military applications.

Key Strengths:

- **Advanced Mobility**: Boston Dynamics is known for creating robots with superior mobility and agility. Their robots can navigate complex terrains, handle obstacles, and operate in environments that are challenging for wheeled or stationary robots.
- **AI and Machine Learning Integration**: Their robots leverage AI to learn and adapt to their environments. For instance, Spot can autonomously navigate through construction sites, mapping and inspecting

in real-time.
- **Unique Application Areas**: Boston Dynamics' robots are employed in non-traditional applications, such as **search and rescue, military surveillance**, and **environmental monitoring**.

Leading Customers:

- **Google**: Google's parent company **Alphabet** acquired Boston Dynamics for its cutting-edge robotics technology, including **robotic logistics** and **AI-powered mobility**.
- **NASA**: Boston Dynamics has worked with NASA on developing robots like **RoboSimian** and **Rover**, which can perform exploration and maintenance tasks in space.
- **Dematic**: Dematic has partnered with Boston Dynamics to integrate **Spot** into their **automated warehouse solutions**, helping with tasks such as **inventory tracking** and **facility inspection**.

Job Prospects:

- Boston Dynamics offers positions in **robotics research, software development, hardware design**, and **robot integration**. Careers in **AI and machine learning** for autonomous robots and **robot maintenance** are growing areas.
- Engineers with expertise in **robot mobility, robot vision systems**, and **AI programming** will find exciting opportunities at Boston Dynamics, especially as the company continues to expand into industrial and commercial sectors.

Conclusion:

These leading companies offer unique opportunities for professionals looking to enter the field of robotics. Whether you're an engineer specializing in automation, a software developer working on AI algorithms, or a technician skilled in robotic maintenance, there are diverse career opportunities in the robotics industry. The future of industrial robotics is bright, with increasing demand for experts in fields such as **robot programming, AI-driven robotics, human-robot collaboration**, and **robot integration**.

As robotics continues to evolve, so too will the opportunities for skilled professionals in the industry.

15

Upcoming Startups

Upcoming Robotics Startups in Singapore

1. Razer (Singapore)

Razer is traditionally known for gaming hardware, but its **Razer Innovation Lab** has been developing robotics solutions for automation and logistics.
  Major Offerings:

- **AI-Driven Robotics**: Razer's innovations in robotics are focused on **AI-driven systems** for automation in logistics and warehousing.
- **Robotic Arm Solutions**: They are exploring applications for **robotic arms** for gaming, entertainment, and consumer interaction.
- **Collaborative Robots (Cobots)**: Razer is also looking into **collaborative robots** to work in partnership with human workers in the gaming, entertainment, and retail sectors.

Key Strengths:

- **Tech Synergy**: Leveraging its experience in gaming technology, Razer has a unique advantage in applying **real-time processing** and **augmented reality** (AR) for robotics applications.

- **AI Integration**: Their deep involvement in **AI** and **machine learning** makes their robots smarter, enabling them to learn and adapt in dynamic environments.

Leading Customers:

- **Logistics Companies**: While specific customers aren't public, their robotics systems are expected to cater to **logistics**, **retail**, and **gaming** industries, all of which are looking for automation solutions.

Job Prospects:

- Opportunities in **AI development**, **robotics programming**, and **automation** integration are on the rise. As Razer continues to push the boundaries of automation, they will be looking for experts in **robot vision**, **machine learning**, and **real-time systems**.

2. HiNT (Singapore)

HiNT is a Singapore-based startup specializing in **autonomous mobile robots** (AMRs) that are primarily used in **logistics** and **material handling**.
Major Offerings:

- **Autonomous Mobile Robots (AMRs)**: HiNT designs and develops **AMRs** that can autonomously navigate industrial environments, particularly for material handling and goods transportation.
- **Robotics-as-a-Service (RaaS)**: HiNT offers a subscription-based service model for businesses that need robots without heavy upfront investment, enabling scalable automation.

Key Strengths:

- **Focus on Logistics**: HiNT's robots are highly effective in warehouse and

logistics applications, reducing human labor and increasing throughput.
- **Autonomous Navigation**: Their robots are equipped with **advanced navigation systems** such as **LIDAR** and **SLAM** (Simultaneous Localization and Mapping) for real-time decision-making.
- **Cost-Efficient**: HiNT's **RaaS model** makes high-end automation affordable for small and medium enterprises (SMEs), democratizing access to robotics technology.

Leading Customers:

- **Logistics & Retail Companies**: They have partnerships with logistics providers and retail chains that need efficient **material handling** and **delivery systems**.

Job Prospects:

- As the company grows, **robotics engineers**, **AI developers**, and **data scientists** with expertise in **autonomous systems** and **logistics** automation will be in high demand. Opportunities for **system integration specialists** and **robot maintenance technicians** are also likely to increase.

3. LocoMobi (Singapore)

LocoMobi is an up-and-coming startup that focuses on **autonomous robotics** for **mobility solutions** and **transportation logistics** in urban environments.
Major Offerings:

- **Autonomous Delivery Robots**: LocoMobi develops autonomous robots for last-mile delivery, particularly in urban environments. Their robots are designed to navigate sidewalks and interact with humans in public spaces.

- **Autonomous Mobility Solutions**: They are working on robotic vehicles that can transport goods across **urban landscapes** without requiring human drivers.

Key Strengths:

- **Urban Mobility**: LocoMobi's focus on autonomous vehicles in cities places it at the intersection of robotics and urban mobility. Their systems are designed to solve logistical challenges in **crowded cities**.
- **Advanced Robotics for Last-Mile Delivery**: They use **AI and computer vision** to ensure their robots can safely navigate pedestrian-heavy areas and deliver goods efficiently.

Leading Customers:

- **Urban Delivery Services**: Their technology is in use by **delivery services** in **Singapore** and other Southeast Asian cities.
- **Retail and E-Commerce**: Companies in the **e-commerce** space are exploring LocoMobi's robots for last-mile delivery solutions.

Job Prospects:

- As a growing company, LocoMobi offers positions in **autonomous vehicle development, robotics software engineering, data science,** and **urban mobility research**. Career opportunities also include **AI-driven navigation systems** and **robotic operations management**.

Upcoming Robotics Startups in India

4. Ather Energy (India)

While primarily known for its **electric vehicles (EVs)**, **Ather Energy** is expanding its technology to integrate robotics for manufacturing and maintenance in the EV industry.

Major Offerings:

- **Autonomous Assembly Lines**: Ather is working on developing **automated production lines** for assembling their **electric scooters**, using robotics to optimize the manufacturing process.
- **Robotics in Service Centers**: They are also integrating **robots** into their **service centers** for diagnostics and repair of electric vehicles, improving efficiency and service quality.

Key Strengths:

- **Sustainability and Innovation**: Combining robotics with sustainable electric vehicle production gives Ather a competitive edge in both **green technology** and **automation**.
- **Focus on Automation in Manufacturing**: They are reducing human error and increasing efficiency through the use of **automated robotic arms** in their **assembly lines**.

Leading Customers:

- **Indian Consumers**: Their EVs are used by customers across India, particularly in **urban areas** with high interest in sustainable transportation.

Job Prospects:

- As Ather Energy expands, there will be increasing demand for **robotics engineers** with expertise in **automated manufacturing**, **AI-driven robotics**, and **electric vehicle maintenance**.

- Positions like **system integration engineers**, **R&D specialists**, and **robotics application engineers** will be key roles at Ather.

5. Graviton (India)

Graviton is an Indian startup that focuses on building **intelligent robots** for industrial applications like **welding**, **cutting**, and **assembly** in sectors like **automotive** and **electronics manufacturing**.
   Major Offerings:

- **Robotic Welding Solutions**: Graviton provides **automated robotic welding** solutions for manufacturing industries, focusing on **precision welding** and **part assembly**.
- **AI-powered Robotics**: They incorporate **AI** into their robots for better decision-making, enhancing the robots' ability to handle complex tasks autonomously.

Key Strengths:

- **AI-Driven Performance**: Graviton's robots are empowered with **machine learning algorithms** that allow them to learn and adapt in real-time, enhancing production efficiency.
- **Customization**: The company specializes in offering **customized robotic solutions** tailored to the specific needs of their clients, particularly in the **automotive** and **electronics** sectors.

Leading Customers:

- **Automotive Manufacturers**: Graviton's robotic welding and automation systems are used by major automotive manufacturers in India for **body assembly** and **precision welding**.

65

- **Electronics Manufacturers**: Companies in the **electronics sector** use Graviton's robots for **circuit board assembly** and **quality control**.

Job Prospects:

- Graviton offers positions in **robotic engineering, AI and machine learning development, automated system design**, and **robot integration**. As a growing startup, they offer exciting opportunities for professionals in the **robotics** and **AI** space, particularly those interested in working with industrial automation.

6. 3Dprintler (India)

3Dprintler is an Indian robotics startup specializing in **additive manufacturing** and **3D printing** technologies, which are integrated with robotics for applications in **production lines** and **product prototyping**.

Major Offerings:

- **3D Printing Solutions for Robotics**: 3Dprintler combines **robotics** and **additive manufacturing** for creating **customized robotic parts** and **tools** used in industrial production lines.
- **Rapid Prototyping with Robotics**: Their robots are used to rapidly prototype parts for the **automotive** and **aerospace** industries, reducing production costs and time.

Key Strengths:

- **Synergy of Robotics and 3D Printing**: By combining robotics with 3D printing, 3Dprintler is revolutionizing the way industrial robots are designed and deployed.
- **Cost-Effective Prototyping**: They enable manufacturers to quickly test and deploy robot parts using 3D printing technology, reducing the need for expensive molds and tooling.

Leading Customers:

- **Automotive and Aerospace Manufacturers**: 3Dprintler works with companies in the **automotive** and **aerospace industries** that require rapid prototyping and custom parts for their robotic systems.

Job Prospects:

- 3Dprintler is actively hiring for roles in **robotics, additive manufacturing**, and **R&D**. Career opportunities include **robotics engineers, 3D printing specialists**, and **material scientists**.

Conclusion

The robotics ecosystem in **Singapore** and **India** is rapidly growing, with startups creating exciting innovations in automation, AI, and robotics. These companies offer unique career prospects for professionals in **robotics engineering, AI development, system integration**, and **industrial automation**. As the demand for intelligent automation systems continues to rise, skilled workers will be crucial to the growth of these startups, making this an exciting time to enter the field of robotics.

www.ingramcontent.com/pod-product-compliance
Lightning Source LLC
LaVergne TN
LVHW081804050326
832903LV00027B/2081